JESUS IN THE DOCK

Robert Kirkwood
and Graham Claydon

Illustrated by Edward McLachlan

To Rev. Sam Tumwesigire,
Peninnah, Timothy,
Christine and Kevin Paul

Acknowledgements

We are indebted to the Bible Society for permission to reproduce Bible text from the *Good News Bible*. © American Bible Society, New York, 1966, 1971 and 4th edition 1976, published by The Bible Societies/Harper Collins.

We are grateful to the following for permission to reproduce photographs: Bridgeman Art Library/Christie's London, page 11 *above*; Church Missionary Society, page 10 *above*; Courtesy of the Trustees of Dartmouth College, Hanover, New Hampshire, USA. Copyright © 1986, page 9 *below*; Ewan MacNaughton Associates (The Daily Telegraph plc) page 28; Sonia Halliday Photographs, page 9 *above* (photo: Andre Held); Mansell Collection, pages 4, 10 *below*; The National Gallery, London, page 5; Carlos Reyes, page 31; © Geoff Ward, page 23 (2).

And to the following people for allowing us to reproduce photographs of themselves on page 11: Christie Archer, Graham Claydon, Grace Hallworth, Anita Naik, Sarah Nutcombe, Jeremy Webb, Jan Young, and the two gentlemen.

Published by
Longman Group Limited
Edinburgh Gate, Harlow,
Essex, CM20 2JE
and Associated Companies throughout the world.

© Longman Group UK Limited 1990

All rights reserved. No part of this publication may be reproduced, stored in a retrieval system, or transmitted in any form or by any means, electronic, mechanical, photocopying, recording or otherwise, without either the prior written permission of the Publishers or a licence permitting restricted copying issued by the Copyright Licensing Agency Ltd, 90 Tottenham Court Road, London, W1P 9HE.

First published 1992
Fourth impression 1995

ISBN 0 582 04581 9

Set in 14/16 point Gill Sans
Produced by Longman Singapore Publishers (Pte) Ltd
Printed in Singapore

The publisher's policy is to use paper manufactured from sustainable forests.

CONTENTS

Did we kill a man sent to us by God?   4

Background to the case   5
Was this man from God?   5
Where does the evidence come from?   6
What did he look like?   8
A problem child?   13
Jesus goes missing   14

The trial begins   15
Jesus: a megalomaniac!   16
Acted just like God   18
Talked just like God   19

The Defence opens its case   21
A megalomaniac: no way!   22
This man came from God   26

The Prosecution continues   30
His message is crazy   31

The Defence replies   35
You've missed the point   36
This is the point   37
Follow the signposts   38
Forgive   39
Don't judge   39
Make peace   40

The Prosecution continues   42
The mind plays tricks   43

The Defence replies   45

Was this man from God?   48

Did we kill a man sent to us by God?

This man is dying slowly. He is nailed to the cross. He is known as Jesus of Nazareth, or Jesus Christ.

This happened nearly 2000 years ago. Jesus is being crucified because he had been found guilty of falsely claiming to be God's messenger. However, not everyone agreed that what Jesus said was false. Those who were his friends and trusted him believed that by crucifying Jesus people were killing a man sent to us by God.

Background to the case

WAS THIS MAN FROM GOD?

Before being crucified, Jesus was put on trial. He was only about 33 years old at the time. The judges decided that he was an impostor. However, it does not seem to have been a very fair trial because it was rushed through the courts in a couple of days.

This book is going to set up a new trial and you are invited to be the new jury. It will not be a full trial, of course. There will only be time to start it off and allow you to listen to some of the evidence 'for' and 'against' this man called Jesus.

You will not therefore be asked to make up your minds about the accused and deliver either a 'GUILTY' or 'NOT GUILTY' verdict. You will only be invited to listen and think.

WHERE DOES THE EVIDENCE COME FROM?

The evidence we have to go on is found in four documents which can now be found in the Bible.

The first document was probably written about 30 years after the trial of Jesus — around 60 AD. Tradition says that it was written by a young man called **Mark**.

The second document was probably written about 5 or 10 years after Mark. Tradition says that it was written by a Greek doctor called **Luke**.

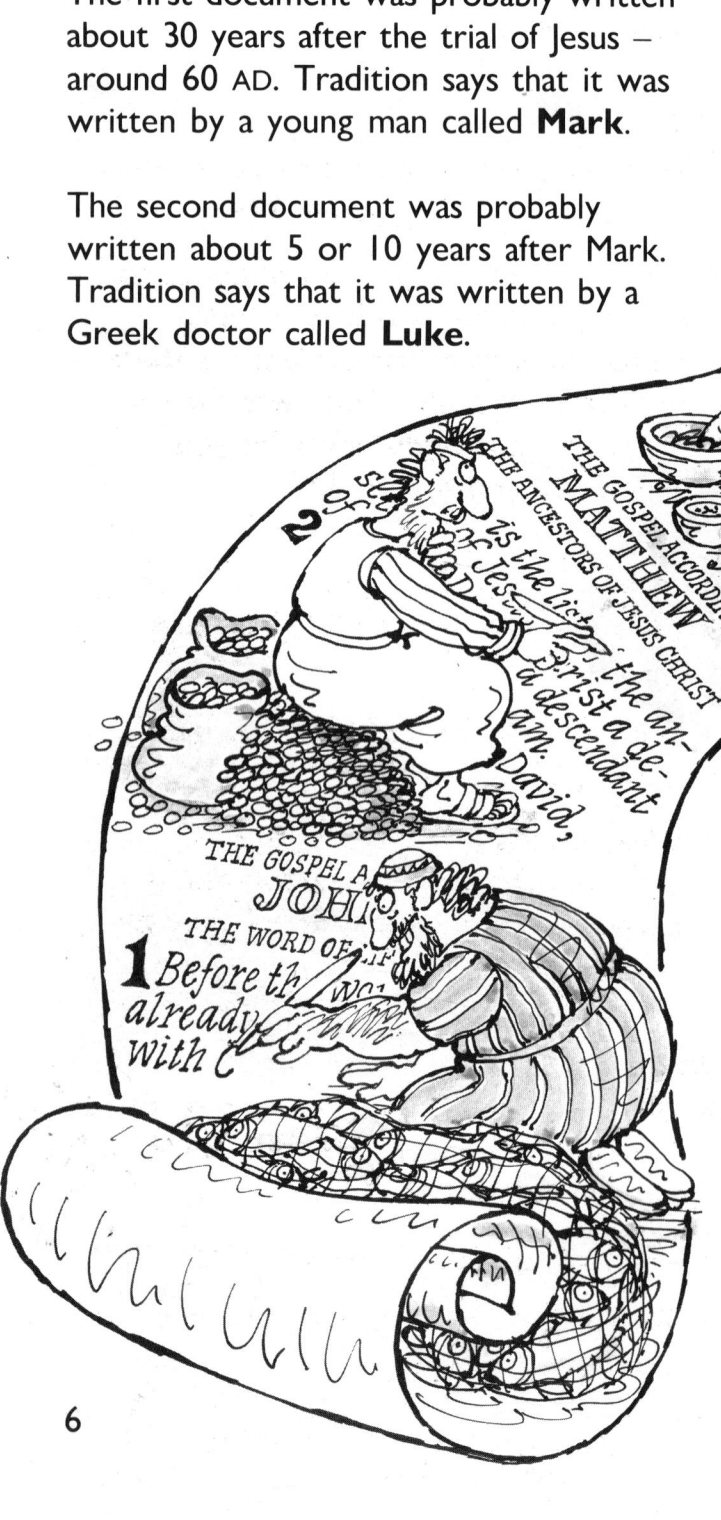

The third document is said to have been written about 10 years after Luke. Tradition says that it was written by a tax collector called **Matthew**.

The fourth document is full of deep thoughts about Jesus and was probably put together by one of Jesus' close friends called **John**. John's friends may have helped him to write it all down. John is the last of the **Gospels**, as these documents are called, and was probably written about 90 AD.

Historians always take seriously documents written as near to the events as the Gospels were. Of course, this does not mean they accept them all as 'Gospel'!

So, members of the jury, you too will be expected to take these four Gospels seriously.

Questions and research

Make Your Own Old Document

1 Choose one of these two methods to make your own old document:

a) Take a piece of sugar paper and cut it to size. Now dab it with vinegar (using cotton wool) to get the 'old effect'. Let it dry.

b) Take the same sort of paper and singe it by placing it on a baking tray and putting it in the oven for about 5 minutes. (This will have to be homework so ask adults to help.)

2 Now write down on this 'old document' some information about Mark, Luke, Matthew and John. Draw pictures to go with this information (perhaps one picture per writer). Your ideas for these pictures should come from the questions below.

Mark

- Some people say that Mark was one of the first streakers. Explain what happened. (Mark 14:51–2)
- Mark caused an argument between two christian friends, called Paul and Barnabas. Explain what this argument was about. (You will need to read the following passages from Acts before finding the answer: 13:5; 13:13; 15:36–40.)
- Paul eventually ended up in prison where he spent a lot of time letter writing. One of these letters makes it clear that Paul and Mark became friends again. What is the evidence for this? (Colossians 4:10)

Luke

- What evidence is there that Luke was well educated? (Colossians 4:14)
- When Paul was in prison and about to be executed, he wrote to a friend called Timothy. What evidence is there from this letter that Luke was the sort of friend who would never let you down? (2 Timothy 4:9–11)

Matthew

- What was Matthew's job? (Matthew 9:9–12)
- What other name did Matthew have? (Luke 5:27–8)
- What evidence is there from the passage mentioned above that tax collectors were looked down upon by others?

John

- What was John's job? (Matthew 4:18–22)
- What were John's brother and father called? (Matthew 4:18–22)
- What was John's nickname? (Mark 3:17)
- Try to figure out why he got this nickname? (Luke 9:51–5)

WHAT DID HE LOOK LIKE?

When a trial takes place the jury usually get the chance to see what the accused person looks like. You, as the jury in this trial of Jesus, won't get this chance. All that can be done is to let you see some paintings. But be warned: don't let these paintings give you either a good or bad impression of the accused. The artists who painted them never met Jesus so all of their ideas about the way he looks are guesswork.

Framed

One of the oldest pictures of Jesus that we have managed to find was painted 200 years after Jesus was executed. It was found in Italy in the city of Rome and so was probably painted by a Roman christian. It was painted on the walls of the underground caves where christians used to meet secretly because the Roman government wanted to get rid of them. These caves were burial places called the **catacombs**.

This picture is of Jesus as 'The Good Shepherd' which was one of the many ways Jesus talked about himself. He seems to be a youthful Jesus with a bit of an Italian pop-star look about him.

This picture of Jesus was painted by a Mexican artist named Jose Orozio. It is called 'Christ and his Cross'. This Jesus has the face of a Mexican. He looks serious, tough and not somebody to mess around with.

Here is a picture showing Jesus being crucified. It is from a church in Uganda and was painted by the African artist Sam Ntiro.

If that picture surprises you, what do you think Africans make of a Jesus like this?

Here are the blue eyes, the blond hair and the white skin of a typical Englishman. But did Jesus look any more like this than the African? Remember, Jesus was actually Jewish!

Probably the most we can say is that Jesus would have looked like most Jews of his day. As a practising Jew he would have had long hair with curling side locks which was part of the Jewish law. He probably had a beard as the Jews liked to appear different to the Romans who ran their country and who shaved.

His clothes are almost certain to have been like any other Jew of his time. Indeed, we read about his long wool tunic in the Gospels. The Roman soldiers diced for it after they had stripped him to crucify him. From the bottom of his tunic there would have been tassels of blue wool. On his feet, like most people at the time, he would have worn sandals.

Questions and research

1 Some people say that you can tell something about a person by looking at his or her face. See if you can match up the faces to the jobs listed in the box. (The answers will come later on.)

> bank cashier; book designer; health visitor; magazine writer; musician; sales rep; storyteller; street seller; vicar

2 Look again at the faces above and try to match them with the words in the list. Compare your results with a person sitting near you. Try to explain to each other what it is about each face that made you match it with particular words. (You may add your own words.)

a) evil
b) trustworthy
c) sly
d) humorous
e) serious
f) good looking
g) snobbish
h) bully
i) nervous
j) gentle
k) friendly
l) unfriendly

3 When artists paint people they often try to say something about the person by painting them in particular ways. Look at the pictures of Jesus in this chapter. Explain what you think each artist is trying to say about Jesus.

4 Is there a connection between the country where the artist lives and the way they have painted Jesus? Explain your answer.

5 When you think of Jesus, what face comes to your mind? Draw a picture to illustrate your answer and then explain:

a) what your picture is trying to say about Jesus.
b) if there is a connection between your country and the way you have drawn Jesus.

6 If it were discovered one day that Jesus had a very ugly face, would it change the way you think about him? Give reasons for your answer.

7 Why do you think that the documents of Matthew, Mark, Luke and John never say what Jesus looked like?

8 Look up Matthew 23:25–8 and explain the connection between the words you read there and the questions you have just answered.

A PROBLEM CHILD?

Juries always like to know as much as possible about any accused person's background. For example, what were they like as a child? Did they get on well with their parents? Did they have many friends? Did they argue a lot, lose their tempers, swear or fight? Answers to this sort of question can often help the jury to understand the evidence that is to come later on in the trial.

Once again, however, you as a jury will be at a disadvantage because the documents of Matthew, Mark, Luke and John tell us very little about Jesus when he was a child. All we have, in fact, is found in the document written by Luke and it is a story of Jesus when he was 12 years old. You, as members of the jury, will have to make do with this.

JESUS GOES MISSING

Each year Jewish families would visit their capital city, Jerusalem, for a special celebration called **Passover**. This happened around their Temple, a place rather like a big cathedral (e.g. St Paul's Cathedral in London). In the document written by Luke (2:41–51) we can read a story of what happened to Jesus when he made one of these visits with his parents.

> Every year the parents of Jesus went to Jerusalem for the Passover Festival. When Jesus was 12 years old, they went to the festival as usual. When the festival was over, they started back home, but the boy Jesus stayed in Jerusalem. His parents did not know this; they thought that he was with the group, so they travelled the whole day and then started looking for him among their relatives and friends. They did not find him, so they went back to Jerusalem looking for him. On the third day they found him in the Temple, sitting with the Jewish teachers, listening to them and asking questions. All who heard him were amazed at his intelligent answers. His parents were astonished when they saw him, and his mother said to him, 'My son, why have you done this to us? Your father and I have been terribly worried trying to find you.'
>
> He answered them, 'Why did you have to look for me? Didn't you know that I had to be in my Father's house?' But they did not understand his answer.
>
> So Jesus went back with them to Nazareth, where he was obedient to them. His mother treasured all these things in her heart. Jesus grew both in body and in wisdom, gaining favour with God and men.

Questions and research

1 Have you ever got lost, run away or wandered off from your parents? Explain what happened.

2 a) If you had done what Jesus did, what would your parents do to you?
  b) Why do you think Jesus got off so lightly?
  c) In Luke 2:50 it says that Jesus' parents didn't understand his answer. Explain what you think it means.

3 This story doesn't tell us much about what Jesus was like as a boy. Try to work out, however, what it might tell you by looking at the words and phrases below and writing down the ones which you think describe Jesus. (You may add your own words.)

a) thoughtless   g) deceitful
b) thoughtful   h) honest
c) curious   i) rude
d) disobedient   j) mature
e) confident   k) religious
f) concerned with doing what is right

4 Now imagine you are Jesus' classroom teacher and write him a tutor's report, using the words from 3 to guide you.

JESUS: A MEGALOMANIAC!

We have already seen that Jesus, when he was only 12 years old, was beginning to act oddly. Remember how he wandered away from his parents for three days; how he could not understand why they were so worried; and how he thought that everything he had done was quite alright...

Well, by the time he was 30 this 'oddness' had turned into madness because like many people who crack up he started to see spirits and hear voices. In the document written by Mark (1:9–11) we read the following:

> Not long afterwards Jesus came from Nazareth in the province of Galilee, and was baptised by John in the Jordan. As soon as Jesus came up out of the water, he saw heaven opening and the spirit coming down on him like a dove. And a voice came from heaven, 'You are my own dear Son. I am pleased with you.'

Hearing this imaginary voice pushed the accused right over the edge. He became a megalomaniac. In other words, he began to talk and act as if he was superior to ordinary human beings and *other* messengers of God.

For example, he began saying that he was so close to God that he was bound to know more about God than anybody else. In John 8:42–7 we read:

> Jesus said to them, '…I came from God and now I am here. I did not come on my own authority, but he sent me. Why do you not understand what I say? It is because you cannot bear to listen to my message. You are the children of your father, the Devil, and you want to follow your father's desires. From the very beginning he was a murderer and has never been on the side of truth, because there is no truth in him. When he tells a lie, he is only doing what is natural to him, because he is a liar and the father of all lies. But I tell the truth, and that is why you do not believe me. Which one of you can prove that I am guilty of sin? If I tell the truth, then why do you not believe me? He who comes from God listens to God's words. You, however, are not from God, and that is why you will not listen.'

Like a typical megalomaniac and know-all he claimed that whatever he said about God was THE TRUTH and that all those who disagreed with him didn't know what they were talking about.

ACTED JUST LIKE GOD

In the document written by Mark (3:1–6) we can read of an argument that Jesus had with some religious leaders. These religious leaders thought that all Jews had a duty to obey ten commandments which they believed had come from God Himself. Number four said: 'Don't work on Saturdays' (a day which Jews call 'the Sabbath'). Jesus, however, went out of his way to annoy them by working!

> Then Jesus went back to the synagogue, where there was a man who had a paralysed hand. Some people were there who wanted to accuse Jesus of doing wrong; so they watched him closely to see whether he would heal the man on the Sabbath. Jesus said to the man, 'Come up here to the front.' Then he asked the people, 'What does our *law* allow us to do on the Sabbath? To help or to harm? To save a man's life or to destroy it?'
>
> But they did not say a thing. Jesus was angry as he looked round at them, but at the same time he felt sorry for them, because they were so stubborn and wrong. Then he said to the man, 'Stretch out your hand.' He stretched it out, and it became well again. So the Pharisees left the synagogue and met at once with some members of Herod's party, and they made plans to kill Jesus.

Now the reason why Jesus thought that his understanding of the Law was right is contained in Mark 2:28:

> So the Son of Man [he called himself this] is Lord even of the Sabbath.

In other words, 'I must be right because like God I am in charge of this Law!!'

TALKED JUST LIKE GOD

Jesus also talked just like God on occasions. For example, in the document written by Matthew (9:1–7), in yet another argument with some religious leaders, he says that he has the right to actually forgive *sins*.

> Jesus got into the boat and went back across the lake to his own town, where some people brought to him a paralysed man, lying on a bed. When Jesus saw how much faith they had, he said to the paralysed man, 'Courage, my son! Your sins are forgiven.'
>
> Then some teachers of the Law said to themselves, 'This man is speaking blasphemy!'
>
> Jesus perceived what they were thinking, so he said, 'Why are you thinking such evil things? Is it easier to say; "Your sins are forgiven," or to say, "Get up and walk"? I will prove to you, then, that the Son of Man has authority on earth to forgive sins.' So he said to the paralysed man, 'Get up, pick up your bed, and go home!'
>
> The man got up and went home.

The only time we get the right to forgive a particular sin is when we ourselves have been hurt by it. When Jesus said that he can forgive 'all' sins he was saying that he has this right because, like God, he is hurt by all the sins of the world.

Members of the jury, if this man is not mad then who on earth is?!!

Questions and research

Megalomaniac

1 What is a megalomaniac? Use a dictionary to find out the meaning of this word.

2 It is sometimes said that *megalomaniacs* are very insecure people. What do you think this means?

3 There are people in all schools who behave like megalomaniacs ('posers', in other words). Try to think of one you know and without naming them describe:

- the way they walk
- the way they talk
- the way they act (especially towards others).

Draw pictures to go with your written answers.

4 Do you ever 'pose'? In other words, do you ever act as if you were the most important person in the world and superior to all others? Explain how or why not.

5 Do you sometimes talk as if you know more than you really do? Give examples and explain why.

6 Jesus claimed to know more about God than anybody else. Explain why. (Read John 12:49–50.)

Acting like God

7 In Mark 2:27 Jesus explains why he disobeyed the Jewish law not to work on the Sabbath by saying:

'The Sabbath was made for the good of man; man was not made for the Sabbath.'

Explain what you think this means.

8 Can you think of:

a) laws in Britain
b) rules in your school

which could be criticised in the same sort of way? In other words, which laws and rules 'are not made for the good of mankind'?

Talking like God

9 Explain why Jesus was said to have 'talked just like God'.

10 In John 8:51–9 Jesus makes another unusual claim.

a) Explain what it is. (Look at verse 58 in particular and then compare what is said here to what '*God*' says in Exodus 3:14.)
b) Explain why this is another example of Jesus 'talking like God'.

Occupations of people shown on page 11:
1 health visitor; **2** vicar; **3** magazine feature writer; **4** musician; **5** bank cashier; **6** street seller; **7** storyteller; **8** sales representative for printer; **9** book designer.

A MEGALOMANIAC: NO WAY

Megalomaniacs claim to be different to other people because they are big-headed. They want everybody to believe that they are the greatest so they walk around talking and behaving as if they are more important than anybody else. They are not the sort of people who go out of their way to care for other people. They may 'use' other people but they don't 'care' for them. They are just too full of themselves for this to be possible.

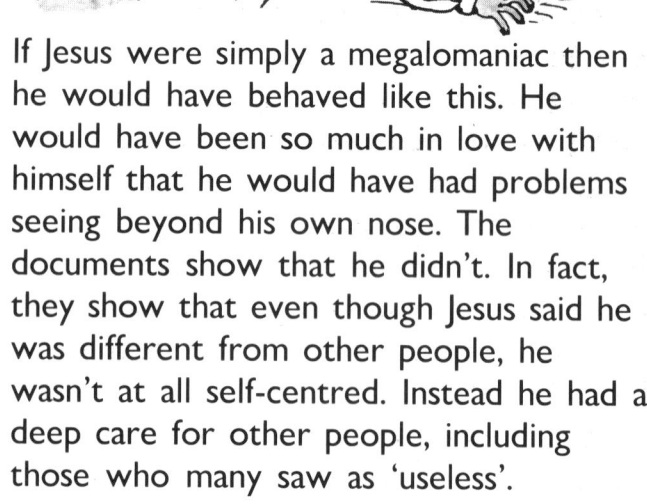

If Jesus were simply a megalomaniac then he would have behaved like this. He would have been so much in love with himself that he would have had problems seeing beyond his own nose. The documents show that he didn't. In fact, they show that even though Jesus said he was different from other people, he wasn't at all self-centred. Instead he had a deep care for other people, including those who many saw as 'useless'.

22

He made friends with outsiders

Jesus went out of his way to make friends with all those who were looked down upon by others. He chose as his friends those who could be of no 'use' to him whatsoever – people who in the eyes of many just didn't count. Is this really the mark of a megalomaniac?

> After this, Jesus went out and saw a tax collector named Levi, sitting in his office. Jesus said to him, 'Follow me.' Levi got up, left everything, and followed him.
> Then Levi had a big feast in his house for Jesus, and among the guests was a large number of tax collectors and other people. Some Pharisees and some teachers of the Law who belonged to their group complained to Jesus' disciples. 'Why do you eat and drink with tax collectors and other outcasts?' they asked.
> Jesus answered them, 'People who are well do not need a doctor, but only those who are sick. I have not come to call respectable people to repent, but outcasts.'
>
> (Luke 5:27–32)

He had time for children

Children are not very 'useful' to people either. They cry a lot of the time, demand your attention and generally tire you out. Some of the disciples of Jesus thought so as well because in the document written by Luke we read that they tried to stop people bringing children to him. Jesus, however, welcomed the children and went out of his way to make a fuss of them. Is this the action of a man who (like a megalomaniac) only wants to get near to people who will be of some use to him?

> Some people brought their babies to Jesus for him to place his hands on them. The disciples saw them and scolded them for doing so, but Jesus called the children to him and said, 'Let the children come to me and do not stop them, because the Kingdom of God belongs to such as these. Remember this! Whoever does not receive the Kingdom of God like a child will never enter it.'
>
> (Luke 18:15–17)

He touched lepers

Leprosy is a terrible skin disease that is caught by 'touch'. In Jesus' day it was incurable. Because it was so easily caught it sent people into a panic every time they came across it and they would run away from lepers. The document of Luke tells us that Jesus didn't run away. Instead he went up to them, 'touched' them and cared for them.

> Members of the jury, it is too simple to call this man a megalomaniac. His behaviour just doesn't fit in with this sort of person. It is clear that we must look for another explanation.

> Once Jesus was in a town where there was a man who was suffering from a dreaded skin-disease. When he saw Jesus, he threw himself down and begged him, 'Sir, if you want to, you can make me clean!'
> Jesus stretched out his hand and touched him. 'I do want to,' he answered. 'Be clean!' At once the disease left the man. Jesus ordered him, 'Don't tell anyone, but go straight to the priest and let him examine you; then to prove to everyone that you are cured, offer the sacrifice as Moses ordered.'
>
> (Luke 5:12–14)

Questions and research

Outsiders

1 Draw a picture or write a poem to show the feelings that you think must be going on *inside* an *outsider*.

2 Have you ever felt like an outsider? Explain when.

3 Have you ever helped to make someone feel like an outsider? Give examples.

4 Do you ever go out of your way to mix with people who are rejected by others? Give reasons for your answer.

5 Look again at the passages you were told to read on pages 23–4 and explain how Jesus behaved towards those looked down upon by others.

Children

6 Have adults ever treated you as if you weren't important? Give examples.

7 Why do you think the disciples didn't want the children coming to Jesus?

8 What was Jesus' attitude to the children?

9 Jesus seems to give children a very special importance because:
a) He warns people not to harm them. What is this warning? (Mark 9:42)
b) He tells adults that they have to become like children. What do you think he means by this? (Perhaps you can answer this question by working out the differences between the attitudes of children and adults.)

Lepers

10 When Jesus cured people of their illnesses he did not always 'touch' them. Think of a reason why he may have chosen to touch the leper.

11 In infant and junior schools, children 'touch' each other a great deal. In secondary schools, many children begin to find touch embarrassing and end up behaving like porcupines. Why do you think this happens?

12 Conduct the following experiment to find out if you find 'touch' embarrassing:

Sit in a circle (next to people you don't know too well) and hold hands for five minutes while having a class discussion on 'touch'. Then answer these questions:

- Did you groan at the thought of doing this? If so, why?
- Did you try to sit next to good friends? If so, why?
- How did you grasp the hands of the people next to you – tightly or lightly as if they were dirty socks?

13 Some people say that if we could only learn to 'touch' each other more then many problems that exist between ourselves and others would be '*cured*'. Do you agree? Give reasons for your answer.

14 Read Mark 9:33–7 and John 13:1–15. Do you think that these passages are evidence that Jesus wasn't a megalomaniac? Give reasons for your answer.

THIS MAN CAME FROM GOD

The documents of Matthew, Mark, Luke and John give us another explanation. They tell us that this man called Jesus was so much 'like' God that he must have come from God himself.

The documents are not saying that Jesus was 'like' God because he 'looked like' Him (as we, for example, might 'look like' our parents). Instead they mean that he had a personality like God and that he possessed POWERS like God. We have already looked at the *personality* of Jesus, now we will look at his POWERS.

His power to control nature

The document of Matthew, for example, tells us of an occasion when Jesus and his friends were in a small fishing boat on Lake Galilee.

> Jesus got into a boat, and the disciples went with him. Suddenly a fierce storm hit the lake, and the boat was in danger of sinking. But Jesus was asleep. The disciples went to him and woke him up. 'Save us, Lord!' they said. 'We are about to die!'
>
> 'Why are you so frightened?' Jesus answered. 'How little faith you have!' Then he got up and ordered the winds and the waves to stop, and there was a great calm.
>
> Everyone was amazed. 'What kind of man is this?' they said. 'Even the winds and the waves obey him!'
>
> (Matthew 8:23–7)

Questions

1 The documents tell of other occasions when Jesus showed that he had the *power to control nature*. Read John 6:1–15 and explain what happened.

2 Jesus often performed miracles in order to help him teach an important truth. Read John 6:26 and 6:35, and attempt to explain the truth Jesus was trying to teach by performing this miracle.

His power to heal

The documents show that Jesus wasn't one of those healers who either had a few lucky breaks or who only healed those with illnesses like colds or sore throats. John tells us that among those who were healed were people who had been blind from birth. One man who received his sight said: 'Since the beginning of the world nobody has ever heard of anyone giving sight to a person born blind. Unless this man came from God, he would not be able to do a thing.' (John 9:32–3)

Question

Read John 9:39–41 and try to explain the truth Jesus was trying to teach when he healed the blind man.

Fiona Marshall, of the Royal Ballet, instructs blind pupils from the RNIB's New College, London.

His power to give life

The documents also tell us that Jesus brought people back to life. For example, in the document written by John (11:32–5 and 38–44) we can read this story about Lazarus.

> Mary arrived where Jesus was, and as soon as she saw him, she fell at his feet. 'Lord,' she said, 'if you had been here, my brother would not have died!'
> Jesus saw her weeping, and he saw how the people who were with her were weeping also; his heart was touched, and he was deeply moved. 'Where have you buried him?' he asked them.
> 'Come and see, Lord,' they answered.
> ... Jesus went to the tomb, which was a cave with a stone placed at the entrance. 'Take the stone away!' Jesus ordered.
> Martha, the dead man's sister, answered, 'There will be a bad smell, Lord. He has been buried four days!'
> Jesus said to her, 'Didn't I tell you that you would see God's glory if you believed?' They took the stone away. Jesus looked up and said, 'I thank you, Father, that you listen to me. I know that you always listen to me, but I say this for the sake of the people here, so that they will believe that you sent me.' After he had said this, he called out in a loud voice, 'Lazarus, come out!' He came out, his hands and feet wrapped in grave clothes, and with a cloth round his face. 'Untie him,' Jesus told them, 'and let him go.'

It was miracles such as these that led many people to ask 'What kind of man is this?' Ask yourself the same question. Jesus' own answer to this question is amazing. However, all the evidence points to this explanation being true – that Jesus, the accused, actually was from God himself.

Questions

Read John 11:25–7 and explain the truth Jesus was trying to teach when he is said to have brought Lazarus back to life.

The Prosecution continues

Members of the jury, if Jesus really were a messenger from God then the 'message' he said he had brought from God should at least make sense. After all, God should know what he's talking about. The problem is, though, that it doesn't. In fact, it's such a load of rubbish that there is just no way that either Jesus or this message could possibly come from God.

HIS MESSAGE IS CRAZY

The message that Jesus said he had brought from God can be found in the document written by Matthew (22:37–9). Jesus says that God wants each of us to be happy in life and that the only way we can be fully happy is to:

'Love the Lord your God with all your heart, with all your soul, and with all your mind.'

Jesus goes on to say that according to God you cannot love Him in this way by simply going to church, reading the Bible and praying. What you have also got to do is to:

'Love your neighbour as you love yourself.'

(Matthew 22:39)

Now to understand why this message is nonsense and could not have come from God you must understand that 'the neighbour' Jesus is talking about is not simply the person who lives next door to you, your family, your friends or even people from your own country. The 'neighbour you must love as you love yourself' can also be a complete stranger and must also include your enemies. Listen to the words spoken by Jesus and recorded in the document written by Luke (6:27–8):

> 'But I tell you who hear me: Love your enemies, do good to those who hate you, bless those who curse you, and pray for those who ill-treat you.'

Do you really think that a God who wants us to be happy would send a man with a message that tells us to become doormats!!!

You may be thinking that I'm being unfair to Jesus and that 'loving your neighbour' doesn't mean allowing them to walk all over you; but that is exactly what he did mean! In the document written by Luke (6:29–30), the following words from Jesus make this clear:

> 'If anyone hits you on one cheek, let him hit the other one too…

> …if someone takes your coat, let him have your shirt as well.

> Give to everyone who asks you for something, and when someone takes what is yours, do not ask for it back.'

Questions and research

1 Jesus tells us to love God by loving our neighbour. Who, according to Jesus, is our neighbour?

2 Have you ever hated and ill-treated another person?

a) Without mentioning names, explain what you did and why.
b) Some people say that when you hate you do more damage to yourself than to the other person. Why do you think they say this?

3 Draw a picture or write a poem to express the feeling of hate.

4 Think of somebody you hate or who hates you.

a) Do you think you could ever follow the teachings of Jesus and begin to 'love' them? (Before answering this question, read 1 Corinthians 13 to get an idea of what christians mean by love.) Give reasons for your answer.
b) If your answer is 'No, I couldn't', do you think that you would nevertheless feel better inside if you could? Give reasons for your answer.

5 Read the following passages and explain how Jesus behaved towards those who were violent towards him.

> John 18:1–11
> John 18:19–24
> Luke 23:32–4

6 Do you think the teachings of Jesus in this chapter make sense? Give reasons for your answer.

The Defence replies

The Prosecution has tried to prove that the message of Jesus is so crazy that there is just no way that either he or this message could have come from God...
Members of the jury, I shall try to show you that this message in fact makes so much sense that it's just the sort that would have come from a God who knows what will make us happy. I shall be saying that this message is further evidence that God has spoken to us through Jesus.

YOU'VE MISSED THE POINT

"I shall begin this part of my case by telling you a short story which I hope will show you what is wrong with the way the Prosecution has understood the teachings of Jesus."

A father took his daughter outside to look at the moon. He pointed with his finger at the great, shiny ball in the night sky and said softly: 'What do you see there?'

The little girl replied: 'Your finger!'

Jesus is like this father because these teachings of 'turning the other cheek', 'giving away your shirt' and 'giving to anyone who asks you for something' are also trying to point out something to us.

The Prosecution, however, has behaved like this little girl. They have simply looked at the teachings of Jesus but have failed to see their point!

THIS IS THE POINT

If we are to see the point of these teachings then we must remember that Jesus was a teacher and like all good teachers he was always trying to grab the attention of those listening to him. He did not have the sort of help that teachers have today: no overhead projectors; no slides; no tape recorders; no videos; no computers and no detentions. All Jesus had was the spoken word. What he often did was to say things in exaggerated ways in order to wake people up and make them listen. When Jesus therefore told people to 'turn the other cheek', 'give away your shirt' and 'give to anyone who asks you for something' he wasn't issuing *commands* telling people that this is how they must behave every time they get a chance to do so – after all, he didn't!

Instead he was deliberately going over the top in order 'to point out' (and this is the point) that if we really want to be happy then we must be ready to make changes to our lives – changes that would mean loving 'ourselves' and our 'possessions' far less and God and our 'neighbour' much more.

Questions and research

1 a) Explain why the teachings of Jesus are said to be like the father's finger pointing to the moon.

b) Explain why the Prosecutor is said to be like the child looking at her father's finger.

2 If you were a teacher, how would you try to get pupils to listen to you?

(Remember that people even switch off when what you are teaching is interesting.)

3 Jesus often used humour to get people listening to him. Read Luke 6:39–42 and then draw a picture to illustrate the example.

FOLLOW THE SIGNPOSTS

If we are going to be fair to the teachings of Jesus then we mustn't see them as 'commands' telling us exactly how we should behave every time we meet another person. Anybody doing that is bound to make them seem a load of nonsense.

> . . . if one of the occupation troops forces you to carry his pack one kilometre, carry it two kilometres.
>
> (Matthew 5:41)

Instead we should see these teachings as *signposts* which guide our love for God and our 'neighbour' in the right direction.

You must decide whether these *signposts* are in fact pointing in the right direction. Are they, as Jesus said, pointing us all to a NEW WAY OF LIFE that will make us more happy? Or are they, as the Prosecution says, leading us up the garden path?... Let us look at more of these *signposts* before you decide.

FORGIVE

Imagine coming to school one day with a new pair of shoes. You bought them because you thought they were fashionable and looked good on you. However, you enter your class and immediately a group of kids start laughing at them and accusing you of looking stupid.

WHAT WOULD YOU DO
OR SAY TO THESE PEOPLE?

Well, the teachings of Jesus don't try to tell you how you should 'exactly' act. Instead they say that if you are to 'love God and your neighbour' then whatever you do or say must be guided by a desire **to forgive**.

DON'T JUDGE

Now imagine coming across a group of your friends huddled together in a corner of the playground gossiping about a girl in your class. They accuse her of being big-headed, a flirt – and much worse. Then they ask you what you think of her.

WHAT WOULD YOU SAY?

Again, the teachings of Jesus don't tell you exactly what you should say. Instead they say that if you are to 'love God and your neighbour' then whatever comments you decide to make must be guided by a desire **not to judge**.

MAKE PEACE

Finally, imagine that two of your best friends have an argument. They say a lot of hurtful things and both decide that they will never speak to each other again. You, of course, are placed in a difficult situation because both of these friends want to sit next to you in class and want to hang around with you at breaktime.

WHAT WOULD YOU DO?

Once again the teachings of Jesus don't tell you 'exactly' what you must do. Instead they say that if you are to 'love God and your neighbour' then whatever you decide to do must be guided by a desire to be a **peacemaker**.

We cannot prove to you that these signposts of Jesus are pointing to a NEW WAY OF LIFE that will make you more *happy*. All we can do is to appeal to your 'experience'. In other words, is it *your* 'experience' that you are a happier person when you allow yourselves to be guided by these signposts?

If you can say 'yes' then perhaps you can also agree that Jesus' message is not crazy, but is just the sort that would have come from a God who understands what we need. You may also agree that this message is further evidence that Jesus really is a person who was sent by God.

Questions and research

Forgive

1 Give an example of an occasion when a person (or a group of people) hurt you in some way.

2 Did you look for revenge or did you forgive them?

3 Have you ever broken up with a friend because you (or they) have been unable to forgive? Explain what happened.

4 Would you be a happier person if you could forgive more often? Give reasons for your answer.

5 Some people say 'I'll forgive you, but I'll never forget what you did.' Is this forgiveness? Read 1 Corinthians 13:5 and explain how a christian might answer this.

6 Read Luke 23:32–4. Do you think that Jesus must have been a very special person to be capable of saying these words. Give reasons.

Don't judge

7 Think about the sorts of things you spend your time talking about. Then answer these questions:

- Do you spend a lot of your time gossiping and criticising others?
- Do you often say nice things about people?

Give reasons for your answers.

8 Sit in a circle. Your teacher will ask each of you to pay a compliment to another person in the group. (The compliment should be about their personality and not about the way they dress.) No hint of criticism is allowed. The compliment must be full-blooded.

9 Try to go through a complete day without saying anything horrible about another person.

10 Read James 3: 6–12. Draw a picture to show what this writer says about the '*tongue*'.

Make peace

11 Have you ever faced the problem mentioned on page 40? If so, what did you do?

12 Have you ever been responsible for two people falling out with each other? If so, explain what happened and why you did it.

13 Are you a happier person inside when you follow the signposts mentioned in this chapter? Give reasons.

14 Read Mark 7:18–23. What do you think Jesus means by these words?

The Prosecution continues

Religious people called 'christians' will tell you that God finally made it clear that Jesus was his special messenger by raising him from the dead. As evidence that this happened they point to passages like the one found in John's document (20:11–18).

Members of the jury, these stories are unbelievable because we all know (if our heads are screwed on right) that dead bodies just don't get up and start walking about! These stories could just be bare-faced lies. However, I think they have more to do with 'wishful thinking'. Let me explain.

It was late that Sunday evening, and the disciples were gathered together behind locked doors, because they were afraid of the Jewish authorities. Then Jesus came and stood among them. 'Peace be with you', he said.. After saying this he showed them his side.

Mary stood crying outside the tomb. While she was still crying, she bent over and looked in the tomb and saw two angels there dressed in white, sitting where the body of Jesus had been, one at the head and the other at the feet. 'Woman, why are you crying?' they asked her.

She answered, 'They have taken my Lord away, and I do not know where they have put him!'

Then she turned round and saw Jesus standing there; but she did not know that it was Jesus. 'Woman, why are you crying?' Jesus asked her. 'Who is it that you are looking for?'

She thought he was the gardener, so she said to him, 'If you took him away, sir, tell me where you have put him, and I will go and see him.'

Jesus said to her, 'Mary!'

She turned towards him and said in Hebrew, 'Rabboni!' (This means 'Teacher'.)

'Do not hold onto me,' Jesus told her, 'because I have not yet gone back up to the Father. But go to my brothers and tell them that I am returning to him who is my Father and their Father, my God and their God.'

So Mary Magdalene went and told the disciples that she had seen the Lord and related to them what he had told her.

THE MIND PLAYS TRICKS

There are people who find it difficult to handle life when somebody they love very much suddenly dies – especially when that dead person was their *main reason for living*.

Some of these people are so overcome with sadness that their minds begin to play tricks on them and they start to *imagine* that the dead person is still there with them. They 'see' them around the house, they 'talk' to them and they carry on living as if nothing had changed.

When Jesus died, many of his friends found this very difficult to handle. Jesus was a person they had all loved very much and while they were together he had become their *most important reason for living*.

It is obvious that some of Jesus' friends were so overcome with sadness that their minds began to play tricks on them because they started to *imagine* that Jesus was still there with them. It was these friends who went around telling people that they had 'seen' and 'talked' to Jesus after he had died. They were not, of course, seeing the real Jesus. Instead they were *imagining* he was still there and it was this that allowed them to carry on believing in Jesus as if nothing had changed.

Questions

1 How does the Prosecution explain away those stories which talk of people seeing Jesus alive after he had died?

2 On occasions our imaginations try to make us happy. Sometimes, for example, we *imagine* that somebody fancies us when in fact they cannot stand the sight of us. Think of occasions when your imagination tried to make you happy by imagining that something was real.

3 The documents tell us that many people saw Jesus after he had died. Some say that these people simply imagined they saw him. For example, they saw somebody who 'looked like' him and imagined it was him. Read the following passages and explain why you think they say this.
Luke 24:13–35; John 20:11–18; John 21:1–14

4 Do you think that these passages are examples of people imagining they saw Jesus? Give reasons.

The Defence replies

There are many people who have their 'heads screwed on right' and who believe these stories that Jesus was raised from the dead. They do so because they are sure that in this world the unexpected can happen...

> Members of the jury, I'm sure that many people did only *imagine* that they had seen Jesus. Not all of the reported appearances, however, can be explained away so simply.
> Let me explain.

IMAGINATION?

In 51 AD (less than 20 years after it all happened) a follower of Jesus called Paul wrote a letter to some christians at a place called Corinth saying that up to 500 people had seen Jesus all at once (1 Corinthians 15:3–7. This was not a case of a lonely, frightened person *imagining* a miracle in order to keep going. This is a story of something BIG happening.

And then there are those stories in the documents which talk of particular people having very special meetings with Jesus. For example, a follower of Jesus called Thomas refused to believe the stories that Jesus had risen from the dead. Like the Prosecution he thought these stories were crazy. Here then is an example of a man who had a 'mind of his own' and who does not seem to be the type whose mind would 'play tricks' on him ... and yet something happened to convince him that these stories were true.

> One of the twelve disciples, Thomas (called the Twin), was not with them when Jesus came. So the other disciples told him, 'We have seen the Lord!'
> Thomas said to them, 'Unless I see the scars of the nails in his hands and put my finger on those scars and my hand in his side, I will not believe.'
> A week later the disciples were together again indoors, and Thomas was with them. The doors were locked, but Jesus came and stood among them and said, 'Peace be with you.' Then he said to Thomas, 'Put your finger here, and look at my hands; then stretch out your hand and put it in my side. Stop your doubting, and believe!'
> Thomas answered him, 'My Lord and my God!'

> Jesus said to him, 'Do you believe because you see me? How happy are those who believe without seeing me!'
>
> (John 20:24–9)

But these stories by themselves are not likely to convince you or anybody else today that Jesus was RAISED FROM THE DEAD. After all, we were not there and did not experience these 'appearances' ourselves – we are not likely to either.

We can, however, experience the 'message' of Jesus. In other words, we can take Jesus' advice and allow the POWER OF LOVE to 'power' our lives. When we experience this 'power' ourselves then it no longer becomes difficult to believe stories which tell us that this 'power' overcame the 'power of death' and raised Jesus from the grave.

Questions and research

1 There are other stories in the documents where Jesus appeared to his friends after he died. For example, read Luke 24:36–53 and explain, in your own words, what was supposed to have happened.

2 The Defence says that it was not imagination that convinced people they had seen Jesus. Do you think these arguments are convincing?

3 Why does the Defence say that we should experience the 'power of love' for ourselves?

4 Read 1 John 4:7–8 and explain why followers of Jesus believe that LOVE is so powerful.

5 Christians point out that no other 'messenger from God' has ever before behaved or spoken in the same sort of way as Jesus. They say that Jesus was more than just a *messenger* of God'.

a) Read Matthew 16:13–16 and explain how Christians describe Jesus.
b) Do you think there is any evidence from the documents which backs up what Christians believe about Jesus?

Was this man from God?

This book has come to an end but the trial most certainly has not. In fact, it has only just started. It has simply given you a glimpse of some of the evidence that you would need to see in greater detail. You — as members of the jury — are not being asked to deliver your verdict. That can only be done at the end of a full trial and whether or not this full trial takes place is now up to you.